The Missendens In Camera

including Great & Little Missenden, Prestwood, The Lee & Lee Common, Great & Little Hampden, Great & Little Kingshill, Ballinger and South Heath

by Clive Birch FSA FRSA

QUOTES LIMITED of BUCKINGHAM

MCMLXXXVI

Published by Quotes Limited
Buckingham, England

Typeset set in Plantin and pictures lithographed by
Key Composition of Northampton, England

Printed by Busiprint Limited
Buckingham, England

Bound by J. W. Braithwaite & Sons Limited
Wolverhampton, England

ISBN 0 86023 302 2

FRONT COVER: Before the railway came, travellers took the coach to Rickmansworth. Here in 1910 the old Magnet coach was taken out for an airing, long after the railway had arrived at Missenden. Already, the Buckingham Arms Hotel was offering Pratts motor spirit to the new car-borne visitor, and J. Brown offered 'High Class Groceries and Provisions' in his shop this side of the Crown. A shop had opened on the ground floor of the Hotel. (CS)

Acknowledgements

I am grateful to Susan Cowdy of The Lee for advice, information and for lending me precious family papers, and to James Venn of South Heath for invaluable help, not least by the use of negatives from the S. H. Freese collection; also to Ann Reed of Amersham for other illustrations. My thanks in particular go to Colin Seabright for access to his unrivalled South Bucks postcard collection; to my old friend and photographic *alter ego* John Armistead for releasing pictures from his own collection and carefully photographing others; to Chris Gowing and Janet Fuller of the County Museum, and Ruth Watts of the County Library, for help and access to pictures, and to Buckingham Library for assistance. I owe a particular debt in my study of the area to the patient scholarship of past and present members of the Bucks Archaeological Society.

JA	John Armistead
SC	Susan Cowdy
CL	County Library
CM	County Museum
CS	Colin Seabright
AR	Ann Reed
JV	James Venn
SHF	S. H. Freese

Calendar to the Sessions Records ed Hardy & Reckitt, Bucks County Council, 1936

The Cartulary of Missenden Abbey Vol I & II Buckinghamshire Record Society 1939 & 1955; Vol III, prepared by BRS, HMSO 1962

Concise Oxford Dictionary of English Place Names Eilert Ekwall, Oxford, (4th ed) 1960

Domesday Book: Buckinghamshire ed John Morris, Phillimore, 1978

Early Man in South Buckinghamshire J. F. Head, Wright & Sons, 1955

History and Antiquities of the County of Buckingham George Lipscomb, J. & W. Robins, 1847

A History of Missenden Abbey Elaine Kaye, Missenden Abbey Adult Education College, 1973

History and Topography of Buckinghamshire Sheahan, Longman, 1862

The Lee Conservation Area Chiltern District Council, 1981

The Lee Old Church The Lee Old Church Trust nd

The Missenden Story Great Missenden Society nd

Post Office Directory of Northamptonshire, Huntingdonshire, Bedfordshire and Buckinghamshire Kelly & Co, 1864 and 1887

Records of Buckinghamshire Bucks Archaeological Society, 1863 to date

Royal Commission on Ancient Monuments, Buckinghamshire (South) 1912

Victoria History — Buckinghamshire ed William Page, 1925 reprinted Dawsons of Pall Mall 1969

If earliest man barely touched the Misbourne valley and surrounding hills and vales, his successors did — axeheads, blades, scrapers and a fair sprinkling of hand-worked flint flakes have been variously found at both Missendens, Hampdens and The Lee. A Roman presence is harder to verify, and the Saxons apparently came late.

Two Old Stone Age relics suggest passing hunters; the Middle Stone Age is better represented and there is ample evidence of Neolithic and Bronze Age activity; a scatter of surface flakes at Great Missenden may mean a small settlement, but it is unlikely. From the 250,000 year old axe head found at Great Missenden to the Bronze Age dagger of 4,000 years ago discovered by The Lee School, the scene was set. But the Romans kept away — true, a second century Cypriot lamp was dropped at Little Missenden, and someone lost three coins at Town Farm, (two Roman and one Greek), while pottery fragments at Great Missenden offer a tantalising glimpse of civilisation, but antiquarian claims for Roman earthworks in Brays Wood and Castle Hill are unproven. Like those in Reddingwick, they are probably medieval at the earliest.

There are earthworks at Oaken Grove and Hampden Park, Great Hampden; Rook Wood and Frith Hill, Great Missenden and the much discussed and possibly Iron Age rampart and ditch boundary known as Grim's Dyke crosses the top of the valley.

If Grim's Ditch is however, Saxon — and it may well be — there is little other evidence of an early Saxon presence in or near the Misbourne. The first sign of settlement is in Domesday — the great Norman survey of exactly 900 years ago.

When William's surveyors ledgered the nation, Saxon estates at Hampden, Little Missenden and Great Missenden were in Norman hands. Before 1066, Sired held Missenden from the Crown; Wulfgeat, Little Missenden from Bishop Wulfwy, while Wigot, and Sired's man Seric held some land there too; Baldwin occupied Hampden thanks to Archbishop Stigand.

Only Wulfgeat hung on — Normans replaced the rest — and Walter Giffard was one of the most powerful: he acquired Great Missenden. He was one of William's counsellors, and it was his grandson, another Walter, who approved his tenant and lord of Peterley Manor, William de Messenden's foundation of an Abbey. At the time, the village was producing half its pre-Conquest income, with nine families running six plough teams for themselves and two for their overlord, with the help of two slaves and a smallholder. There was substantial woodland, feeding 500 pigs. The village probably held some 42 souls. Little Missenden was home to perhaps 32, and Hampden up to 20.

Missendene is a Domesday term, but the word derives from the Danish *mysse* or water arum; delightfully *Messebourne* means 'stream where the water arum grew'. Hampden appears in Domesday too: 'valley with a village'. The Lee — Leia, La Lega, Leye, Leie — is a 12th century term from the earlier *leah*, or clearing, open ground. Kingshill is obvious; Prestwood suggests 'wood with a priest'.

The Manor of Lee was not mentioned in Domesday, but belonged to Bishop Odo. Originally a chapel of ease to Turville, Lee Chapel was granted to Missenden Abbey by Geoffrey de Turville in the 13th century. Little Missenden was split into five estates. Hampden's Norman lord was

Osbert, from whom the Hampden family claimed direct descent. Little Hampden was administratively part of Hartwell.

The area first came together in association with the Abbey. This was a small foundation for under twenty canons of the Augustinian order of Benedictines from Arrouaise in France. The actual date of foundation is arguable, but most agree on 1133. The 1330 Missenden Cartulary recorded that Giffard, second Earl of Buckingham, confirmed William of Missenden's church foundation and allocated its income to the Abbey. Another charter confirms the Abbey foundation — but it is possible that the canons had already colonised the site beforehand.

The Abbey had its own church, refectory, chapter house, cloister and dormitory. It was surrounded by gardens, a fishpond, and a locked precinct wall. By 1180 its incomes had increased. An Abbot's lodging was built. In 1247 Henry III, who was a frequent visitor from his palace at Brill, gave timber from his Royal forest at Bernewood for a new guest house. This was Buckinghamshire's first and one of its wealthiest Abbeys, amply endowed with churches and their tithes and with its own library, three volumes from which survive.

But in 1236 Bishop Grosseteste reprimanded the Abbot for mismanagement and lack of devotion. By 1281 the Abbey's affairs were in a mess. The King put in two outside managers to clear the debts and reorganise the farm. In 1297 Bishop Sutton was worried about suicidal tendencies and matters reached their nadir in 1416, when Abbot Ralf Marshall was convicted of counterfeiting and clipping the coinage at his manor of The Lee. He was sentenced to death, but later reinstated.

In the 15th and 16th centuries, all monastic rule was relaxed. Here, there were rows between Abbot and canons. In 1518 Bishop Atwater admonished the latter for day trips to the village, and their butler for insubordination. Bishop Longland's man Jackman in 1530 found that bailiff John Compton was running the entire operation for his own profit, and that one canon, John Slythurst, was 'verbose, of elate mind, and a sower of dissension'. He was also a paederast — and there were children being schooled at the Abbey. He was confined to his cell. Longland, a busy man, nonetheless made a personal visit a year later, when he found that Abbot John Fox and canon Roger Palmer were both having affairs with a married woman in the village — Margaret Bishop. Palmer had his own keys, and took himself off when he felt like it after dark. And he discarded his habit for 'doblett and a jerkyn with a swerde by his side'. He was gated. The Abbot was suspended. Longland was so disgusted that he wrote his lengthy instructions in English: 'for that ye be ignorant and have small understanding of Latin we have drawn our said Injunctions in our vulgar English tongue'. Money and morals were both in a mess — on an annual turnover of £390, the Abbey was trading at a £50 loss.

A porter was appointed, a teacher sought, children in care limited to six and no women admitted. The canons were to stay put, and not to wear 'courtly fashioned' clothes. Fox got his job back. This was a time of Protestant protest, and one Missenden miller, 'Father' Roberts, was burnt at the stake in Amersham. Over 20 villagers were force-marched there, carrying faggots for the fire. The Abbey was designated a place of pilgrimage for penitents — at the shrine of 'Our Lady of Missenden'.

Came the Dissolution. The Abbey was valued at

£261 14s 6d and dissolved in 1538. Everyone got a pension (Fox was dead) and Slythurst became Vicar of The Lee. By 1554 Canon Thomas Bernard was Vicar of Missenden — and married. Courtier Richard Greenway leased the buildings and estate. In 1560 Richard Hampden took over, but 14 years later the whole lot went to the Queen's favourite, Leicester, and he promptly sold it — to William Fleetwood, whose staunchly Protestant family kept it for two centuries.

The Lee passed to the Russells until the 17th century Plaistowes acquired it. Peterley Manor, which had gone to the Abbey in 1141, was granted to Geoffrey Dormer, remaining with the family into the 20th century. Little Missenden was released from Bicester Monastery.

Henry VIII's itinerant surveyor John Leland described Great Missenden thus: 'It is a praty Through-fare, but no Markett Towne'. Yet it could have been. Local life centred on the Abbey but Henry III granted a market and fair. It was not taken up. By the 13th century there was a watermill at Great Missenden (Deep Mill) and by 1352 at Little Missenden. In 1367 Thomas de Mussenden was granted a confirmation of a weekly Tuesday market and an annual fair, later held on Easter Tuesday and the Monday after Michaelmas, but abolished in 1883. From 1234 to 1257 land was granted from the Abbey estate to Peter Pottarius, and there is a 13th century reference to Le Pottererewe. Opposite Park Farm, two separate sites have thrown up medieval and 17th century pottery including early unglazed pots and 14th and 15th century glazed jugs, jars and bowls. By 1535 'Pott, Rewe and Balenger' are recorded Abbey lands and in 1560 the Crown granted Potterrowe and Ballynger to Richard Hampden.

Courts were held in Great Missenden as early as 1254 and the lords of the manor held rights of gallows, pillory and tumbril. While travellers of note stayed at the Abbey guest house, others needed accommodation in the village. The George was built around 1483 probably alongside the original court house. The Red Lion was the only other major inn, joined in the 16th century by the Buckingham Arms.

If the valley was previously untroubled by the outside world, it was rudely shattered by the actions of John Hampden — John the Patriot. First he refused to pay his taxes — 20s Ship Money on a local parcel of land near Honor End Farm. Then he raised a regiment of foot for Parliament, and finally he lost his life, after an injury, at the battle of Chalgrove Field. There can be little doubt the Puritan cause echoed round these hillsides.

In 1679 Elizabeth Cellier (née Dormer) was accused of high treason. Known as 'the Popish mid-wife' she was said to have conspired against the King's life, suborned one Dangerfield at Newgate where she was a prison visitor, and to have concealed the evidence in a tub at home — hence 'The Meal-tub Plot'. She was acquitted, but convicted of libelling the prison authorities, and fined £1,000 with three appearances in the pillory. She died within the year and was buried in the chancel at Great Missenden Church.

While the Dormers and others were in trouble for their Catholicism, Joseph Graveney of Prestwood in 1689 registered his house for Quaker meetings. A year later Matthew Axtell was up against planning restrictions: he appeared in court to explain his 'new erected cottage'. Two years after that, John Moores of Great Missenden was granted a £2 pension for faithful military service, and in 1693

Francis Clarke of Great Missenden refused work offered by the overseers of the poor, unless it was above the ordinary wage. Plus ça change . . .

Within a century, nonconformity had pervaded the area. Ballinger Common had its own Baptist Chapel in 1776; Great Missenden two years later. The 'establishment' was less fortunate, for the Hampden estate was halved by government action, after the Patriot's great grandson unwisely and illegally invested Naval Treasury funds in the 'South Sea Bubble'.

In 1787 the 5,727 acre Abbey estate was sold to James Oldham Oldham, a City ironmonger, who rebuilt the Abbey. By now windmills had appeared above and down the valley — at Frith Hill, and two at Little Missenden. At Harvingfield, near The Lee, the eccentric Major Thomas Backhouse was buried at his express wish, upright with his sword beside him, in a flat topped pyramidal mausoleum in the woods. In 1807 his son moved him into the church.

In 1806, the year Ballinger Baptist Chapel was enlarged, Oldham sold the Abbey estate to stockbroker John Ayton, who rebuilt it yet again, in its present Gothick style. Oldham endowed Missenden's school by the green in 1822, the year he died, leaving £400,000. Ayton sold on in 1815 for £44,000 to George Carrington, a West India sugar planter. The Carringtons stayed for four generations. The year before, Little Kingshill Baptist Chapel was built.

By 1826 the 19th century AA Guide — *Paterson's Roads* — gave the Missendens only one entry, as on the road from London to Shrewsbury *via* Wendover and Aylesbury. The turnpike of 1847 and modern coaching practice changed all that. By 1862 Great Missenden was described as 'delightfully situated in a valley . . . on the high road from London.'

In 1833 Missenden acquired a workhouse — behind the George, where every other Monday the Petty Sessions were held. Five years later, the town's Baptist Chapel was replaced, the same year Ballinger's was declared unsafe and rebuilt. Prestwood Parish was created in 1849, when both church and school were opened.

Ballinger Common was enclosed in 1852 and the Great Missenden enclosure award was dated 1855 — when today's field boundaries were defined. In 1862 Joseph Birch owned Ballinger Grove. In 1864 a daily coach from Wendover to London collected passengers at 7.30 am and returned at 8 in the evening.

Great Missenden's trade and commerce was extensive: it included two straw bonnet makers (Fanny Bong was one), six shoemakers, two saddlers, a tinplate worker, a watch and clockmaker and bell hanger, chair turner William Hart, two blacksmiths, two wheelwrights, a carman and a carrier, surgeon (George Smeathman), plasterer, milliner, miller and innkeepers. No mention of the George.

The Old Church at The Lee was finally replaced (but preserved) by the 'new' church in 1868. In 1872 Great Missenden School was rebuilt Four years later Lee Common had its National School. Meanwhile in 1875 Missenden's fire service had been inaugurated, with its own horse-drawn manual pump, kept at the Plough, by the corner of Church Street. Lee Common was enclosed in 1883, and one year after that Great Hampden obtained a National School. South Heath was a 19th century enclosure of manorial wastes.

By 1887 the London coach had become an omnibus, returning twenty minutes later than in 1864. Now it only ran in the summer. Missenden pubs were listed as the Buckingham Arms, Crown, Lamb, Plough, White Lion,

Barley Mow, George, and Red Lion. The last four have survived, together with the Black Horse, Cross Keys, Waggon and Horses and the Nag's Head. New trades included John Stroud, bird stuffer, two fancy repositories, painters and decorators, a marine store dealer and cattle dealer Israel Pearce.

In 1892 the Hampdens were combined in one parish, there was a Primitive Methodist Chapel at Lee Common, and the railways came. In 1889 the new transportation brought London into Metroland, with the main London-Chesham line; in 1892 the Metropolitan Railway bought up the Buckinghamshire Railway (Aylesbury to Verney Junction), and linked Rickmansworth to Aylesbury, thus pushing Chesham onto a branch link, and bringing Missenden 'on line'. Two years later, widow Carrington switched on the electric street lamps in Great Missenden — and one year after that the town switched them off in favour of oil. It may have had something to do with a local firm — British Volta Electric Glow Lamp Co. (It was not until the late '20s that electricity came back.) That same year the Parish Council replaced the ancient parish Vestry, and in 1899 they provided a public water supply.

As the new century dawned, the Plaistowes of The Lee sold out to Arthur Lasenby Liberty, son of a Chesham draper, and his Chartridge wife, Rebecca. Liberty was a man of vision, with an acute eye for colour and texture. He travelled worldwide to build up his Regent Street business acquired in 1875, but yet had time for home. He transformed the Manor House, created the Green in 1901, built the old Guildroom in 1903, rebuilt the Cock and Rabbit on a new site in 1907, and gradually bought up the entire parish, save one farmer's land. While Liberty was improving, so was Missenden PC, with a new water supply in 1902, and in 1913, the girls' school.

By 1938 the Carringtons were gone — Squire George and his four sisters had dominated local life from the '90s but the last two girls died in 1938 and the Abbey was inherited by Maj Thomas Temple-Carrington. After the war he sold out to the County. In June 1947 the Adult Education College opened its doors. In 1953 the Stewart-Liberty family sold The Lee estate to meet death duties.

In the post-war years, electrification to Amersham, diesel trains to Aylesbury, the opening of motorways like the M1, M4, and M40 have all served to intensify pressures on the Chilterns, and to encourage speculative building. Traffic pours ceaselessly down the hillsides and along the valley. Modern development has been somewhat constrained — there is little on the church side; The Lee is a conservation area, and Ballinger not over-infilled. The Kingshills and Prestwood have borne the bulk of the rurban spread, while the Hampdens have escaped it and Missenden itself has acquired some good and some not so good public and private buildings. A modern private hospital facility prospers in the Little Abbey, for a time a hotel, but the Abbey itself, closed in 1984 for extension and repairs, was destroyed by fire in July 1985 — the estimated damage to this Grade I Listed building by an act of arson was £1.5m. The gutted shell is shored up with steel, a new building has been constructed, and opens in 1986 as part of the Missenden Abbey Management Centre. Meanwhile today's commuters jostle yesterday's natives, the new canons of this 'praty' valley, colonising where property values will surely never go down, and nothing too unpleasant will ever go up.

Appropriately, Will Barnes wrote in 1909 'I arrived here, safely had a shower or two. I found all well . . .' and he stayed at the Black Horse, Mobwell or Mob's Well Great Missenden — the source of the Misbourne, the stream round which the Missendens grew. (CS)

Along the London Road, at the entrance to High Street West, stood the imposing elm trees, Matthew, Mark, Luke and John (and their companions) — they are reflected in today's Elmtree Green, and associated with Elmshurst, the Dormer mansion which replaced Elmridge, the family house and which in 1887 was a 'Ladies' Boarding School' run by Elizabeth Crawley. (CS)

The Post Office was well established in Great Missenden by 1847. In 1864 Miss Emma Willmore was in charge: 'Letters from Amersham at 7.20 am& 3.45 pm; dispatched at 8.55 am& 5.20 pm.' In 1917 it looked like this. (CS)

The view from outside Elmshurst at the beginning of our century is one of entire tranquillity as children play in High Street, and Mrs Mann's cook at Elmshurst, Maud from Deddington, writes 'have a lot to do just now . . . (we have) not got a parlour maid yet.' (CS)

Within two decades, change is evident: traditional transport stands outside the Cross Keys in the 1930s, while the motorcar crowds the highway further down, and three tea rooms jostle the inns and shops for the visitors' custom. (AR)

George Oakes at the White Lion, established 1858, offered livery for your horses, stables, bait, and choicest rooms in his 'noted house' — Missenden High Street East also boasted Burton's Restaurant a little way down on the right, and beyond that the Red Lion and the Crown, c1900. (CS)

Obviously a man of his times, Oakes soon converted the stables into what he advertised as 'Livery Stables and Motor Garage' — well patronised, to judge by these five early vehicles, BH 2167 on the right complete with chauffeur. (CS)

Further down High Street East, the Red Lion (Wheeler's Ales & Spirits) offered counter attractions — billiards, Livery and Bait, Stables for 'open & closed carriages' — while the milk cart, complete with churn, passes the tobacconist on its leisurely way through a lightly trafficked town. (CS)

At the turn of the century, in Church Street, leading off High Street, painter, glazier and plumbers Henry and Joseph Ingram stand opposite an ironmonger's shop, with the Church in the distance, just below the brow of the hill. (CS)

Church Street exhibits a calm and untroubled face, with the 17th century Swan pulbic house opposite H. J. Wright, carpenter, whose one-horse four-wheeled open cart carried the legend 'Builder & Contractor'. A. Osborne, local newsagent and stationer, printed this card at the close of the last century. (CS)

The original water supply has survived into modern times at the corner of Church Lane: well, pump, and horse trough were provided by the recently formed Parish Council in 1899. (CS)

The Schools, c1905: James Oldham Oldham, Citizen of London, ironmonger, owner and rebuilder of the Abbey, endowed the school by the Green from his £400,000 estate the year he died — 1822. Seventy years later the school was rebuilt. In 1913 the girls' school was built. The 'Oldham' school is now the C of E primary school. (CS)

Church Lane gives way to Church Path, and Church Gate, leading up the hill to the Parish Church of St Peter and St Paul, of 12th century origin on an earlier Saxon site. Today it is reached by a bridge over the 1960 bypass. (CS)

The tithes of the Church were granted to the Abbey in 1133. The building is Early English, with 17th century bells, a Decorated nave and windows in the Perpendicular style. The registers date from 1678. (CS)

As High Street East continues past Church Street to become again the London Road of yore, the originally 1483 George reflects its significant complementary role to the Abbey guest house, as Missenden's oldest secular hostelry — in this early 20th century view from High Street stationer, J. H. Spittles. (CS)

Behind the George lay the 16th century Court or Sessions House, where manorial courts were held, and then the Petty Sessions, every other Monday. Magistrates' Courts were held fortnightly at Missenden into the post-war era. It may be that the original building on this site was once the guild hall for the community. (CM)

At the end of last century, the gateway to the ancient Abbey had been somewhat facelifted, the walls provided a convenient leaning post, and cattle were driven in leisurely fashion down the London Road. Life was clearly conducted at a sensibly tranquil pace. (CS)

The Abbey founded in 1133 by William de Missenden, and confirmed by his overlord, Walter Giffard, became one of Bucks' wealthiest houses, and passed to the Fleetwood family after the Dissolution; centre of Missenden's life, it became James Oldham's home in 1787, was rebuilt, sold to John Ayton in 1806 and rebuilt again, went to the Carringtons in 1815, and became County Council property in 1947. Fire gutted the building in 1985. (CS)

The Misbourne, from which Missenden gained its origin and its name, once flowed through the Great Abbey Park in rural tranquillity — and with a great deal more presence than today, when the water table has been lowered by modern demands. (CS)

Warren Bridge crossed the Misbourne at the entrance to the Abbey Park, the ford a convenient watering hole for local cattle, and a hazard to horse-drawn transport. Today the ford and bridge are gone; the stream is culverted beneath the earth. (CS)

These cottages at Clark's Lane, entrance to today's Misbourne secondary school, opposite the Abbey entrance, were about to be demolished in this picture of 1935. (SHF)

Little Missenden Abbey, latterly a hotel and now the hub of a modern private hospital facility, was said to connect with the Abbey proper by underground passage; no passage exists, and the building was never an abbey. (CS)

London Road wends its muddy way towards Little Missenden, the Nag's Head the last outpost of civilisation; Mr Wright's cart stands beside the pub as building debris is sent down the chute, and a horse trough is conveniently placed opposite. (CS)

Between the two Missendens, Deep Mill was recorded in the 13th century — here at the turn of the century it wears a dejected air; in 1887 William Clarke was the miller. This card carries the jaunty message 'Doesn't this look a nice cool place?' Today the mill is no more, but its name lingers on in Deep Mill Lane, and for many years a filling station nearby advertised weekly: 'DMFSLMOOS' — known throughout the area as 'Dumfusselmoos — Deep Mill Filling Station, Little Missenden, Open on Sundays.' (CS)

Suffolk's Bridge spans the Misbourne on the road between Great and Little Missenden. The fishpond here was too far away from the Abbey to be the usual monastic facility, but by the 19th century it had become a useful food source for parishioners. (CS)

Founded in the same century as Great Missenden's church, the Parish Church of St John the Baptist, Little Missenden, is still substantially a 12th century structure dating to c1120, though the chancel was remodelled in the 13th, and the tower is 15th century, the oldest bell of the 14th century. Its registers date back to 1559. The tithes were granted by Gilbert Bassett to Bicester Monastery in 1182 'for the good of his own soul, that of Egelina his wife and those of his children'. (SHF)

In 1931 Professor Tristam uncovered wall paintings in Little Missenden Church, with St Christopher the dominant figure. (CM)

At the juction of the village road — The Street — and the Holmer Green road, now a private house, were the Village Stores and post office run by James Garraway in the 1880s, and William Olliff in 1864. The post arrived at 8 and left at 4.30. (CS)

The Manor House, opposite the churchyard, is an 18th century and Victorian modernisation of a late 16th century building — the estate for which it was originally built was one of five feudal holdings in Little Missenden, this one known as Beamond Manor. (CS)

The Red Lion was run in 1864 by William West — a John West was the village wheelwright at the time; James Plumridge was the landlord in 1887. In this 1910 picture from Garraway of the Post Office the main promotion is for Leadbetter's V.O.S. Whisky. Weller's Entire Ales were the staple product. (CS)

In this earlier, c1888 view of The Street, with the Red Lion in the background, and the church and manor beyond, school is clearly just out — the school itself was founded in 1830 for 110 children, with Maria Nichols mistress when this picture was taken: her mother preceded her 25 years before, when she was assistant mistress. (CS)

Missenden House, Little Missenden is a finely proportioned building, described in 1860 as 'a handsome red brick residence, very pleasingly situated in about five acres of pleasure grounds etc . . . (it) contains a good collection of paintings, oriental china, valuable and rare carvings in oak, and numerous articles of vertu collected both at home and abroad by its present owner and occupant, Captain John Otway Cuffe'. He was still there in 1887, by which time the 'collection' had accrued 'an antique Greek lamp', dug up at Cnidus in Caria by Dr Blaxall of HMS Vigilant. (CS)

The Crown offered 'Good Accommodation' and 'Teas Provided' in this 1931 picture, when Frederick Kingham was landlord and Weller's Entire Ales on offer. Mr Kingham and his wife stand behind the ubiquitous horse trough — in use even then. Fifty years earlier Mrs Caroline Clayton ran this house, and before her, Isaac Pitt was landlord. (CS)

The Spring, Little Missenden offered a cost-effective means of cleaning your cart in 1900, and a source of unending fun for local children, like the two tucked away by the edge of the footpath here, complete with their miniature buckets — for catching freshwater crayfish, perhaps? (CL)

Little Missenden's water and steam mill in 1935 — earlier known as Sibley's Mill, the Old Mill and now as The Mill House. In the inter-war years, it was sometimes lyrically called 'the old mill by the stream' (at Amersham!). John Sibley was the late 19th century miller and farmer. In 1864 William Clarke, 20 years later the miller at Deep Mill, operated what was then only a water mill — Sibley installed steam. (CM/JV)

Thankfully, this scene of the 'backs' at Little Missenden has remained substantially unchanged, save for an unfortunate pair of corrugated grain silos on the roadside — since Mr Garraway took this picture around 1910. (CS)

The steam link between Rickmansworth and Aylesbury speeds through Little Missenden. At one time the only connection was by coach, for the original 1889 line went direct from Aldgate to Chesham, while the Buckinghamshire Railway linked Aylesbury and Verney Junction. In 1892 the 'Met' opened their new Extension Railway from Chalfont and Latimer station to Aylesbury — via the Missendens. (SHF)

High Road, Little Kingshill — and time to exchange gossip over the garden fence on the edge of the unmade road c1900. In the last quarter of the 19th century, three farms were the only listed commercial establishments at King's Hill — and two of them had gone by the end of the century. (CS)

Little Kingshill Schools, pictured here at the turn of the century, existed in the 1880s, with accommodation for 60 boys and 60 girls; Miss Emily Phillips was mistress; it was not there twenty years previously. (CS)

Little Kingshill Common presents a bare and forlorn face to the early 20th century photographer. The village was known in the 18th and 19th centuries as the hamlet of Kings(e)hull — simply a collection of farms and 'respectable-looking cottages' — largely bypassed by the railway era, but finally caught up in the age of the motorcar. *(CS)*

The Red Lion at Great Kingshill where the common land was enclosed in 1853 — until then the area was open common land. In 1862 the 70 homes were described as 'mostly modern' and 'several of which are very neat'. This picture was taken in the mid-1920s. (CS)

In 1926 Ian R. Purdie specialised in pedigree Middle White pigs at Cherry Tree Farm, Great Kingshill. His Bandora herd included this brood sow — clearly a champion. (CS)

Peterley Manor c1900; the 1840s Dormer family mansion was demolished and this fine house built on the site. Originally part of the Abbey estates, from 1141, the estate went to the Dormers on the Dissolution — the original house was erected in 1616. (CS)

'This is the pond where the butterflies are' wrote Mrs Knotley to her son Fred, at home at Wandsworth, in 1911. Collingshanger Pond at Collings Hanger Farm, on the edge of Prestwood, clearly relied on pondwater and stacked a neat rick or two. (CS)

Monopolies are nothing new as Amersham's Weller brewery well knew — here the bold advertisers at the Chequers of Prestwood, where the contemporary 'road' was little more than a muddy track, single carriage at that. John Tompkins was a 19th century Prestwood beer retailer — possibly the forerunner business to this public house. (CL)

Prestwood's Church dates to 1849, when the new ecclesiastical parish was formed and both church and school built. Originally Prestwood formed part of the Abbey's lands at Great Missenden and was the 17th century estate of Sir Edmund Hampden, whose family died out in 1741 with Henry Hampden of Honor End, churchwarden in 1726. (CS)

Prestwood has a non-conformist pedigree stretching back to Joseph Graveney, whose house was registered for Quaker meetings in 1689; the Wesleyan Chapel has since acquired a central window. (CS)

L. Morren of Prestwood published this 1900 scene of the High Street, dominated by his own stores, and post office, complete with public telephone — a far cry from today's bustling thoroughfare. (CS)

This Edwardian Prestwood Carnival photograph was possibly taken at Green Lane, where clearly the major event was the children's fancy dress competition. The picture was with others in a family collection found in an Amersham house — the family was Benthall. (AR)

Prestwood yielded stone for the restoration of Windsor Castle in the 19th century, and clay for brickmaking. Here the clay diggers pause for the camera in the late 1890s, at Solomon Groom's brickyard, Kiln Common, Prestwood. Inset: Solomon Groom himself. (CM)

Samuel Howard's brickyard at Prestwood employed a horse to turn the pug mill in 1927. The pug machine mixed and aereated the clay before the bricks were laid under straw to dry out prior to firing. (CM)

The monument to John Hampden was erected at Prestwood in 1863 near Honor End Farm. There are three other memorials — at Chalgrove Field, where he died, at Stoke Mandeville and in Aylesbury. The site is allegedly on the field for which he was taxed the 20s Ship Money he refused to pay. (CS)

At the top of Martins End Lane, Grimms Hill now bristles with favoured properties — in 1905 it was sparsely developed, and notably, trees were planted as houses were built; those same trees have long since reached respectable maturity, proving that modern landscaping has something to learn from our Edwardian forbears. (CS)

Martins End Lane just about accommodates a single horse and trap in the early 20th century — today's traffic has created a demand for less hazards and more carriageway. As motorists sit and fume on their way home from the station to the intensely developed hinterland of Prestwood and the Kingshills, let them close their eyes and remember this lost country lane. (CM)

The White Lion livery stables were the most prominent advertisement in the station yard outside Great Missenden Station; the timetable was hard by the entrance, headed Great Central Railway — a reflection of the Metropolitan & Gt Central Joint Railway — the GCR went from Missenden to Sheffield; the local Met train was but two carriages and a tender. (CS)

Leading westwards from Missenden, and leaving London Road opposite Elmshurst, the highway passes Rignall Farm on its way to King's Beech and Hampden Bottom. In 1774 Rector John Mosse wrote in Great Hampden church register: 'Eerly in ye spring in 1774 the Springs made their appearance in Hampden bottom, and rose to a far greater height than in 1764. From below the Gravel-Pits thro' West Field, a large stream of water, thirty feet wide, bent its course by Riggnall, during . . . March, April and May, and emptied itself into the Mob-Well.' It had last happened 110 years previously. (CS)

The Old Pepper Boxes in Hampden Bottom, at the foot of the glade leading to Hampden House — in fact the original lodges to the House where lived John Hampden — 'the Patriot' — cousin to Cromwell, Member of Parliament, and martyr to the Puritan cause in the Civil War. (SC)

Hampden House itself is of 14th century origin, with major 18th century additions and alterations. The family claimed descent from Osbert, son of Baldwin, holder of the estate before Domesday — in 1753 the male line died out and the estate went by marriage to the Trevors — who promptly changed their name to Hampden. In 1824 that line died out, so the estate went to the Hobarts, descended from the same Hampden of 1753. In 1849 it happened again, and the estate went sideways, to a brother. The house eventually became a school, then a film studio, and in 1986 offices. It was sold in January 1986 for £600,000 to Marlow Underwriting Agency. (JA)

The galleried hall of Hampden House earlier this century was, to say the least somewhat crowded; family portraits vie with game trophies, militaria and the surfaces are covered with family papers, photos and objets vertu. (CM)

Great Hampden Church of St Mary Magdalen includes many Hampden family memorials, and is principally a 14-15th century structure with 12th century origins. Hampden was buried there, disinterred in 1828, and reburied. (SC)

Great Hampden Rectory is a 16th century house, refaced with new brick in the 18th century and enlarged in the 19th. The timber framed original had a single, central chimney. The approach to the Rectory was originally a carriage drive from near the Common — this 19th century view of Rectory Lane was earlier known as Hampden Street. (CS)

In 1860 the houses in what was known as Hampden Row were scattered farmsteads and cottages beside the Common. 'The supply of water is at all times meagre' wrote one historian, 'and the cattle are watered at ponds' like this one — Blakemoor Pond on the Common, which took its name from Blakemore Farm. (CS)

Little Hampden Church boasts a medieval timber framed porch and a 12th century nave — the building was substantially restored in the 18th and 19th centuries. Until 1892 the church was a daughter church to Hartwell — then it was merged into Great Hampden Parish. (SC)

On Hampden Common the Rising Sun — another Weller house — was run by George Brown towards the end of the century. Farmer John Thompson was landlord in the 1860s. (CS)

At the turn of the century these chair bodgers or turners were at work in Hampden Woods, on the Hampden family estate. Theirs was the skill that made the so-called Windsor chair, thus named because it was marketed in the Royal town. (CS)

The Old Thatched Cottage, at Hunts Green on the edge of The Lee parish — in a not so tidy state in this evocative 19th century study, before modernisation. (CL)

The original church at The Lee, now known as The Old Church and undergoing restoration through a local trust, was built in the 13th century of clunch. It has curious window glass: the east window contains the figure of John Hampden, supported by Cromwell and Miles Hobart — and surmounted by a fragment of 13th century glass. The 'Cromwell' glass was originally given by Arthur Lasenby Liberty, to Great Hampden Church, but the Earl of Buckinghamshire was having no Cromwell in his church, so back it came, and ended up here. This 1875 painting by William Callow RA shows the church with its long-gone tower. (SC)

The present Church of St John the Baptist was built in 1868 for the sum of £1,300. Its bell came from the old church and dates to 1290, the work of Michael de Wymbis. Originally the parish was a chapelry to Weston Turville, granted to Missenden Abbey, hence the hamlet's old name, Lee Chapel. (SC)

This early 20th century view of the entrance to The Lee reflects some of the changes Arthur Lasenby Liberty had wrought, including the Guildroom meeting place on the left, now a private house, and the creation of the Green, complete with railings. The new Cock and Rabbit is in the centre of the picture. (CS)

The new Cock and Rabbit looks firmly established and properly 'period' in this 1930s picture. 1208588 Aircraftman Second Class Ronald Macers wrote on the back in April 1941 'Have been billeted at the above. Having a grand time.' Presumably he was serving at Halton Camp. Today's customers would certainly echo his joyful sentiments. (CS)

Before Liberty recreated the Green, and on the site of today's War Memorial, there stood this ancient and decrepit range of buildings, creating a dangerous corner opposite the Manor House. The buildings were the original Cock and Rabbit. (SC)

The triangular Green, neatly posted and chained, complete with Memorial, and properly fenced with extremely desirable residences, has matured since Liberty's ministrations, in a view taken in the late '20s. The glaciated sandstone rock dug up in the village and mounted on a pedestal by Liberty is just out of the picture. (CS)

Arthur Lasenby Liberty bought The Lee Manor and estate in 1900. He acquired the entire parish save for the Bassibones farms, and wrought many improvements. His family still live in the village, but alas, the house is sub-divided into four, a product of the 1953 estate sale to meet the exigencies of death duties. The house was 'Liberty Hall' when this 1920s photograph was taken. (SC)

This charming interior of the drawing room at The Lee Manor contains paintings which have gone to America, and furniture now much dispersed, but one table — the kidney occasional piece in the centre — is still in the family, and in the village. The extraordinary 'flamingo' lamp is typical of Liberty's eye for style and rarity in design. Miss Kate Morris in c1938 had something to say about the domestic arrangements at the Manor; she was the cook. In a series of letters entitled The Chronicles of The Lee, she commented: 'The Lee Manor consists of more passages, short steps, dark Hidey holes & lobbies than I have been elsewhere'. (SC)

3 September 1912 and Arthur Lasenby Liberty and his wife Elaine pose for the camera 'on the occasion of the Marriage of their niece'. The camera belonged to the Royal photographer, W. S. Stuart, who held warrants to the King, Queen, Queen Alexandra, and the monarchs of Spain, The Hellenes and Sweden. (SC)

Once a year Liberty invited his Regent Street shop staff to the Manor. They came by train to Missenden, with their families. The lord and lady of the manor pose here with them, with their family around them, behind the central croquet hoop. Three rows back and fourth and fifth to the right are two bearded gentlemen—John and Walter Beeson, local men. The campanile on the roof of the manor was altered in 1903, so this picture must date from the first or second year of the Liberty's residence there. (SC)

Left: Mr and Mrs Baldwin of Erriwig Lane celebrated their 50th wedding anniversary the day this picture was taken at the turn of the century. The Baldwins were of ancient lineage and originally a Cholesbury landowning family. It is said that Mr Baldwin would return from Aylesbury Market in pony and trap, having enjoyed a suitable refreshment, and beat Mrs Baldwin. (SC) Right: Four William Hollands reflect four generations of natives. William senior farmed the Manor lands; his son William on his left was head gardener, while his son William Arthur was in charge of the electrics. The Hollands served on the Parish council and Flower Committee. Wm junior — William Maurice (the baby here) is a part time churchwarden and still lives at The Lee. (SC)

The ladies of The Lee, 1920s: Back row left to right — Mesdames Clark, Eldridge, J. Bignall, Miss Liberty, Mesdames Lloyd, Oliver, Jacobs, Austin, A. Hearn, Langston, Sills, Head and G. Witney; centre — Mesdames Humphreys, F. Pearce, Parker, Lily Langston, Adams, Evans, Hance, Mrs Stewart-Liberty and Mrs Deaney; front — Mesdames Morris, Dutland, Delderfield, R. Pearce, A. Randall, Bonham and Hedges. Only 15 years earlier, local women still carried on straw-plaiting at home. (SC)

Left: The timber for extending and improving The Manor, and for the Regent Street shop extension were from HMS Impregnable, bought by Sir Arthur; he also bought this figurehead of Earl Howe, its commander, and planted it on the roadside. Every year Frank Pearce has painted it for half a century. (SC) Right — In 1914, local lads joined up 'For King and country' and bivouacked temporarily at The Lee. (SC)

The Church School, The Lee, in 1905 seemed a pleasant place to learn the '3 Rs'. The girls dressed individually but the majority wore uniform smocks over their day dresses. Attendance was around 90. (JA)

In the early 1920s, Will Piddington took the tenancy of the Liberty estate's Church Farm; prior to that he worked at Strawberry Hill Farm, where this photo was taken, complete with three-horse plough team. The Liberty estate in 1909 stretched from one field east of Brays Wood to three fields west of Dutchlands Farm, and from one field north of Jenkins Hill on Hogtrough Lane to the field this side of Redding Wick Wood in the south. Field names on the estate included Conscience, Praters Furlong, Gingerbread Field and Joseph's Piece. (SC)

Left: In 1897, Queen Victoria's Jubilee was marked by sinking the Jubilee Well at Lee Common. The Common was enclosed in 1854. It was 365 feet deep — ie to the depth of Ballinger Bottom, and at the Opening Ceremony a little girl, later Mrs Dwight, was lowered the full depth of the well, here under construction. (JA) Right: The Browns built the well: inside is Harry Brown, in front, his son Frank, right another member of the family, and left Ezra Hawkes. This picture was taken by Mrs Lasenby Liberty in April 1900. William Pearce used to take a bucket of water to the top of Swan Bottom Hill, next to Docwra's, for a penny a time: (SC)

The Baptist Chapel at Lee Common later lost its tower and porch and acquired two dormer windows; here it is pictured c1900, after Sunday School. It was recorded in 1862, and is now privately owned. The occupants nonetheless keep the gravestones in good order. (JA)

Oxford Street, Lee Common in the '20s, with Cllr G. Lewington in the doorway of his premises, Postman Wag Nash with bike and boater, Eddy Pearce sitting on the wall, Joe Humphreys and behind, Geoff Pearce with Bunny, and Lily Talmer with Winnie. Mr Palmer sits on the left with Madge Pearce, Mrs Palmer and Mabel Pearce; and Gertie, Harold and Ralph Rodwell. (SC)

Today trees and hedges obscure this view of Ballinger Bottom; the fields here were the only part of the Parish not forming part of the Liberty estate. The gradient was steep enough for horse transport to need the human brake — a lad behind the wheel as the carter pauses for breath. (JA)

The Post Office at Ballinger around 1905 has since lost its bay window and gained a plate glass front, a kiosk and wall-box. When this card was mailed there on Christmas Eve 1908, the writer, Mary, wrote that 'my dwelling place is . . . on the other hill . . . rather dull.' (CS)

Geo. H. Hunt ran the Bakery and General Stores c1905 and published this picture of the Pond; today the track is grassed over and the pond itself smaller and overgrown. Clearly in those days it was used as a watering hole for horses and cattle. (CS)

The Bull offered teas, and a pony and trap for hire in the early 1900s. Two windows remained blocked up since the days when Window Tax was imposed. The Chesham Brewery dray is making a delivery in this picture by George Hunt. (CS)

Bury Pond, Potter Row provides the backdrop for the postman on his rounds in this late 19th century study; the cart tracks mark where horses were taken to water. Potter Row was recorded in the 13th century — in 1234 land here was granted to Peter Pottarius, and tangible evidence has been found of a medieval pottery. (JA)

The Lamb public house at Potter Row, no longer in business, receives a visit from the baker's cart in the early 1900s. It was a Weller house. (SC)

In the 1870s William Callow RA painted a number of scenes in the Missenden area. Here he recorded for posterity the cottages opposite the Lamb at Potter Row — in July 1876. (SC)

Today we have difficulty discriminating between Romanies and 'didicoys' or latterday tinkers. We complain about the litter on our roadsides and lay-bys. Yet we admire the original Romany 'vans of yesteryear. Here at Potter Row in 1935 S. H. Freese caught the genuine article, complete with horse, and the family neatly dressed and with a decidedly smart perambulator. (SHF)

S. H. Freese lived at The Kraal, King's Lane, and among many photographs he took of 1930s agricultural equipment is this wonderfully evocative study of timber waggons passinng his house, on the way to the Chesham Road and (probably) Jesse Wright's mill at Chesham. (SHF)

The women worked the fields at harvest time, while the men drove the three horse team, and the farmer stood by with his single barrel shotgun to catch the rabbits as their cover vanished — a valuable additional food source — here in Beeson's Field, to the rear of Hundridge Farm Cottages off Mill Lane, before the Barley Mow. (CS)

In 1935 the cottages beside the Barley Mow beyond Frith Hill were demolished. The pub was a Simonds house, and also sold pigfeed at the time. In the late 19th century Henry Kempster was landlord, and before him, Ephraim Parsons in the 1860s — a Parsons ran the Chequers in Great Missenden at the time, and doubled as bricklayer. (SHF)

Mill House stands in gardens which were once the site of Missenden's windmill, off Mill Lane. The mill itself was recorded by 1787 — as was one at Little Missenden. Prestwood's mill lasted ten years and burnt down in c1860. The mill was burnt down in 1876, the year after William Callow painted it. It appears to be a copy of the mill at Lacey Green (originally above Skottowe's Pond at Chesham, in Lowndes Park), which was itself the oldest known smock mill; thus, Missenden's mill may also have been among the earliest built. (SC)

Frith Hill was described in 1847 as 'a lofty eminence . . . with its varieties of wood land and tillage, the windmill on its summit . . . and extremely picturesque.' As it became later with Dell Cottage and the Glen. The then track to The Lee can be seen on the extreme left of the picture. (CS)

Today the by-pass runs through this field, where in 1934 the harvest was reaped in Bury Fields, Reading's Farm. The haywain is drawn by a two horse team. (SHF)

Before the railway came to Missenden, letters had to be conveyed to railheads elsewhere — Berkhamsted for one. They went by mailvan, and in the mid-1930s the remains of the last vehicle lay rotting in a field at Beamond End Lane. (SHF)

Tudor traveller John Leland said of Missenden that its Abbey stood in 'a goodly ground about divers pretty hilles well wooded' and, despite the encroachments of development, well wooded Missenden and its district remains — this early 20th century view by Spittles shows the footpath through Stockings Wood. (CS)

The Buckingham Arms, now a bank and the Abbey bookshop, once boasted a Jubilee clock, and the Buckingham Restaurant. It was originally a 16th century building. In the 1920s its oak lounge looked like this — one wonders where customers put their beer, in what by any standards was a cluttered, if homely environment. (CM)

On 18 November 1914 Great Missenden turned out in force for a Royal visit. HM King George V was 'in town' to review troops billeted here; they lined the High Street as he marched past the Cross Keys. The 'good old days' were nearly done, and modern life begun. (CS)

Appropriately we leave the Missendens by the same way we arrived — down the London Road towards Mobwell — by horse and cart past the old Toll Gate House, where the tolls were paid to the turnpike keeper when first the London Road was improved and Missenden found itself, according to Paterson's Roads 'on the way to Shrewsbury'! Happily, this reminder of what communications have meant to the Missendens since the Abbey pilgrims first trod these paths, survives virtually unchanged to the visitor's eye. (CS)

Index to Illustrations

